Look for the other books on weather by

Marion Dane Bauer
Rain • Wind • Clouds

ISBN 0-439-71122-3

Text copyright © 2003 by Marion Dane Bauer.
Illustrations copyright © 2003 by John Wallace.
All rights reserved. Published by Scholastic Inc.,
557 Broadway, New York, NY 10012, by arrangement with
Aladdin Paperbacks, Simon & Schuster Children's Publishing
Division. SCHOLASTIC and associated logos are trademarks
and/or registered trademarks of Scholastic Inc.

30 29 28   13 14 15 16/0
Printed in the U.S.A.   40

First Scholastic printing, November 2004

Book design by Debra Sfetsios
The text of this book was set in Century Schoolbook.

Snow

written by Marion Dane Bauer

illustrated by John Wallace

Scholastic Inc.

New York   Toronto   London   Auckland   Sydney
Mexico City   New Delhi   Hong Kong   Buenos Aires

The winter world is cold.

The trees are bare.

The grass is brown.

Gray clouds crawl
across the sky.

Clouds are crystals of ice.

Each bit of ice
clings to a speck of dust.

The specks of ice and dust
cling to
one another.

They grow so heavy
that they drop
from the cloud.

Snow!

When the air is very cold,
the snowflakes stay small
and bright.

When the air is not so cold,
the flakes grow soft
and larger and larger.

They grow big enough
to catch on your mitten
or on your tongue!

Each snowflake has six sides.

They come twirling
to the earth in a billion
different shapes.

Snow dresses the trees.

Snow covers the grass.

Snow keeps the flowers warm through the long winter.

When spring comes,
snow melts into puddles,

into rivers,

into lakes,

and gives the earth
a fresh, cool drink.

But while winter is here,
snow makes the cold world
beautiful . . .

and so much fun!

Facts about snow:

✻ The temperature has to be thirty-two degrees or colder for water to turn into ice.

✻ Every snowflake has six sides.

✻ Every snowflake can contain as many as fifty crystals of ice.

✻ Trillions and trillions of snowflakes fall in a single storm, but the flakes take many of different forms. People used to think it was impossible to find two alike, but a researcher named Nancy Knight once did find two snowflakes exactly alike.

✻ When strong winds drive heavy snow, we have a blizzard.

✻ Clouds can make snow even in summer, but because the summer air close to the earth is warm, the snow turns into rain by the time it reaches us.

ALSO BY

Marion Dane Bauer

Though you can't see the wind, you can
certainly feel it when the wind blows!
But where does wind come from?
The answer is at your fingertips.
Read about the wonders of wind....

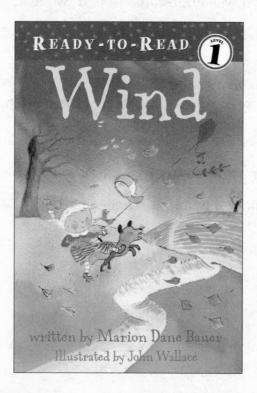